Colin Garratt's Scrapbook
Images from The Transport Treasury
Compiled by Jeffery Grayer

© Images and design Transport Treasury 2023 Text Jeffery Grayer

ISBN 978-1-913893-29-3

First published in 2023 by Transport Treasury Publishing Limited. 16 Highworth Close, High Wycombe, HP13 7PJ

Totem Publishing an imprint of Transport Treasury Publishing.

www.ttpublishing.co.uk

Printed in Tarxien, Malta By Gutenberg Press Ltd.

'*Colin Garratt's Scrapbook*' is one of the books on specialist transport subjects published in strictly limited numbers and produced under the Totem Publishing imprint using material only available at The Transport Treasury.

Front Cover: The first of three locations featured in this volume is the scrapyard of George Cohen, situated on the former Cransley ironstone branch near Kettering. The brutal nature of the scrapman's task is vividly illustrated in this view of a Black Five in the process of being dismembered. The second image records one of the spectacular conflagrations in the "firing shed" at King's/Mayer Newman of Snailwell whilst the third image records the famous locomotive body stack to be seen at Vic Berry's yard in Leicester

Back cover: After the intense heat has done its work, the stout fireproof doors slowly rise to reveal the charred remains of a Class 101 DMU in the incinerator operated by Mayer Newman at their Snailwell facility.

Frontispiece: Whilst a workman sets about the valve gear of a Black 5 at Cohen's yard, the footplate is engulfed in flame as the wooden floorboards are consumed.

Introduction

The renowned photographer, author and publisher Colin Garratt, who died in 2018 at the age of 78, left a remarkable legacy of images of railways around the world. Globetrotting Colin, who earned the soubriquet 'the David Attenborough of the steam locomotive' wrote and illustrated more than 60 books many based on his expeditions to over 40 countries documenting the world's last "working" as opposed to "preserved" steam locomotives before they too became part of history. Whilst he is primarily known for his images of world-wide steam he also covered railways closer to home and had a particular passion for the photogenic opportunities which scrapyards, industrial locations and scenes of railway dereliction afforded. Living a few miles south of Leicester he was well placed to visit Vic Berry's yard and his collection of some 200 images taken here and at King's/Mayer Newman's yard at Snailwell near Newmarket, together with some earlier views taken at Cohen's yard at Cransley, form the basis of this collection.

"Pile 'em high, sell 'em cheap" was the mantra of Tesco founder Sir John "Jack" Cohen and indeed this was the title of his authorised biography published in 1972. Whilst the second part of this quote may not necessarily apply to subsequent sales from locomotive scrapyards, in the case of Vic Berry's yard in Leicester the first part certainly holds true and the famous "stacks" of locomotive and coach bodies came to characterise his premises in the city. Based in the former Great Central Railway (GCR) goods yard at Braunstone Gate to the south of Leicester Central station Vic Berry established his scrapyard in 1973 and in a similar vein to Woodham's yard at Barry he initially concentrated on breaking up redundant BR passenger coaches and goods wagons with the first locomotives, three Class 76 electrics, not arriving until April 1983. There were several elements to Vic Berry's operation as he covered not only the scrapping of redundant rolling stock and locomotives but also specialised in the hazardous business of blue asbestos removal and the refurbishment and repainting of stock prior to a return to operational duties. It was not just BR items that were dealt with as stock from CIE, London Transport and private industry was also handled. Whilst asbestos removal, generally from the cabs of locomotives and from the internal lining of coach bodies, rendered them safe for scrapping it also allowed the yard to sell on stock to preserved railways as it was a requirement of such sales that hazardous material should be removed before a subsequent transfer could take place. This allowed many locomotives to enjoy a second life in preservation which would otherwise have been lost. The firm also won a contract in 1982 to scrap 100 redundant Routemaster buses at London Transport's Aldenham depot although their contract was terminated under something of a cloud before all were dealt with.

Due to the limited nature of the Leicester site perhaps the most famous and visually striking aspect of the scrapyard was the construction of the "stacks" of complete locomotive bodies, severed cabs and coach bodies which, piled three or four high, totalled some 40 items on occasion and was certainly an impressive and photogenic sight. At the end of 1990 following the scrapping of the last complete locomotive the yard went on to handle DMUs and EMUs from many parts of the BR network. Like other scrap dealers, such as the "flying cutters" from Cohen's, staff from Vic Berry undertook demolition work at other sites such as Eastleigh and Swindon Works, Derby and Thornton yard in Fife with severed cabs being subsequently transported to Leicester by road for asbestos removal. Following the closure of the GCR route to freight in 1965 access to the site was afforded by a spur constructed from the Leicester to Burton upon Trent line thus allowing stock to be brought in and wagonloads of recovered metal to be taken away for reprocessing.

In the early hours of Sunday 10 March 1991 a fire broke out in the yard with fire fighters taking several hours to bring it under control resulting in considerable damage to the stock and, more seriously, leading to the release of airborne asbestos across a wide area with citizens being instructed to close their windows. Although never formally determined, the origin of fire was locally attributed to rough sleepers who had been occupying some of the coaching stock. As a result of the conflagration, and of mounting financial problems, the company ceased trading in June 1991 apparently owing a large sum to creditors. The final straw was the inability to reach a deal with its landlord BR for the asbestos decontamination of grounded bodies with BR issuing an ultimatum to the company giving it five days to begin clearing the site and threatening to bring in a contractor to undertake the work. Employing some of his former staff, site clearance was undertaken. However, the closed site was left significantly contaminated from the disposal process. The area was subsequently cleaned up and redeveloped during 1996/7 as part of the Leicester City Challenge project and was named Bede Island with housing and offices today occupying much of the location of the former scrapyard. Although opening too late to accommodate the destruction of BR's steam fleet, the Leicester yard nevertheless played an important role in the disposal of diesel, electric and other rolling stock images of the destruction of which command as much attention amongst today's railway fraternity as did the end of steam to a previous generation.

Another scrapyard which attracted Colin Garratt's attention was that of King's, later Meyer Newman, at Snailwell near Newmarket in Suffolk where many items of BR multiple unit stock met their end during the 1980s and early 1990s. The particular feature on site that caught his attention was the "firing tunnel" into which stock was propelled and then set alight leading to the production of some spectacular images redolent of Dante's Inferno.

Earlier Colin had also visited the scrapyard of George Cohen & Sons at Cransley near Kettering where he was just in time to photograph the destruction of some of BR's steam fleet in 1967 and 1968. I came to know the history of this yard when researching material for my book "Cohen's – A Northamptonshire Railway Graveyard" published in 2018. Cohen's were to handle nearly 300 steam locomotives, both BR and industrial, as well as many diesel locomotives and several diesel and electric multiple units plus a couple of SR Co-Co electrics. Additionally they scrapped a large volume of coaching and freight stock. Their yard near Kettering was situated on the former Cransley ironstone furnaces site and began operations in January 1963 and lasted until the site was cleared in September 1981 at which time it was taken over by a car breaking yard. It has now been redeveloped and all traces of its former role have disappeared.

Jeffery Grayer, Devon 2023

George Cohen & Sons - Cransley

During a visit to the yard on 18th February 1967 Colin Garratt captured Ivatt Class 4 2-6-0 No. 43018 awaiting the inevitable. As this was a Saturday no cutting was taking place and he was able to wander around the yard at will. Sporting a hand painted 5D shedcode, this Ivatt had been withdrawn from Stoke depot in October 1966 and was to meet its end a couple of months after this view in April 1967. Also in shot are an Ivatt Class 2, No.46519, and an ex-LMS Jinty. Unlike many urban scrapyards the rural nature of this yard is very evident in this view with pleasant countryside forming the backdrop. No. 43018 was one of six members of the class and No. 46519 was one of just a pair of the class handled by Cohen's at this location.

A close up of the Jinty reveals it to be No. 47649 which had moved from its Crewe South depot the short distance to Crewe Works in March 1966 although it was not officially withdrawn until that October. It was one of 90 Jintys built in 1928/9 by William Beardmore & Co., a shipping and engineering business of Dalmuir Glasgow, to a Fowler design and was one of twenty-one members of the class to be scrapped here.

Seen through a glassless "office" window where Cohen's workmen doubtless sheltered from the elements and brewed their tea, a foreground of wheelsets leads the eye to a firebox suspended from the gantry of one of several cranes employed in the yard, this example being rail mounted.

Sparks fly as the scrapmen set about their task of wheel cutting. With a suitably fast shutter speed Colin Garratt was able to freeze the action and capture this spectacle on film. The track seen in the background led to the former ironstone workings at Loddington and was, somewhat unusually, opened in 1877 by the main line railway company the Midland rather than, as was more often the case, the quarry operators. This line closed to regular traffic in 1963 upon closure of the quarries although the line was retained for a number of years in the expectation that quarrying would resume. However, this never occurred and the line beyond Cohen's was formally taken out of use in June 1970.

Left: A pair of driving wheels frame some of the red metal gas cylinders found in many a scrapyard. These contain propane. Like acetylene, propane can be used for cutting metal although techniques vary as propane only releases 10% of its heat in the inner flame whereas acetylene releases 40% in its inner flame. Scrapyards tend to use propane for cutting rather than acetylene as cutting quality is of no concern. Behind the crane and shrouded in smoke from burning detritus lie several locomotives awaiting their fate.

Right: Close up of the no doubt laborious work required to sever the many spokes of a driving wheel in order to reduce the scrap to manageable sizes for placing into wagons and onward transport for recycling. In the days before strict Health & Safety regulations, at least protective goggles are being worn by the operator of the torch.

The end result of all that cutting; driving wheel centres, axles and half cut bogie wheels lie in a heap ready for loading.

The process of cutting the smaller bogie wheels into two pieces rather than cutting through all the spokes is shown here. The snaking cables from the gas cylinders to the torch would undoubtedly be considered something of a "trip hazard" in today's safety conscious climate.

Cut wheels obviously had a fascination for Colin Garratt judging by the number of shots he took of them. The contrasting colours of bright and tarnished metal and rust all combine to produce an arresting image.

The procedure for cutting the smaller wheels in half prior to removing the axles is well illustrated here with the driving wheels in the background showing the relative scale of the bogie wheels.

Against a background of piles of scrap, a pair of driving wheels awaits attention.

Discarded rims and spoke sections lie in the foreground as the final few spokes are severed.

Black 5 No. 44851, which was withdrawn from Newton Heath shed in April 1968, was to be found in the yard in August 1968 together with classmate No. 44965 from Bolton depot shortly before the end of steam on BR. The 4-6-0 is evident in the background here as a scrapman sets about cutting the spokes of a driving wheel.

Bending to his task, the scrapman gets to work on cutting a driving wheel.

Removal of the boiler cladding has revealed the lagging underneath. Safety goggles perched on top of his head will not afford the scrapman much protection. Perhaps of more significance is the fact that the boiler lagging of steam locomotives consisted of mattresses of asbestos, the product being used prolifically throughout the 20th century in the railway industry. As a result many people who worked in locomotive construction, maintenance and disposal went on to develop conditions such as asbestosis.

The partially exposed smokebox of a Black 5 reveals that a quantity of char remains from its last revenue earning journey as the activities of the scrapman causes it to cascade down the front of the locomotive. This image dates from 26th August 1968, just a few days after the finale of steam on British Rail.

Perched precariously on top of the remaining half of the front boiler casing, a scrapman sets about extracting the chimney, not by removing the bolts but merely by cutting around the base of the chimney with his torch.

Severed boiler tubes covered in scale make a macabre foreground to the cut up remains of a Stanier Black 5 whose "entrails" are revealed in this view.

A severed Black 5 chimney lies abandoned, awaiting collection and ultimate melting down to fabricate who knows what in another life. These Stanier 4-6-0s were to be the most prolific class dealt with by Cohen's with no less than seventy-three members coming to the end of the road here. This view is dated 25th September 1968.

With his hands protected by a stout pair of gloves, the scrapman, sporting a rather natty red striped shirt and V-necked jumper worn back to front as is his cap, turns his attention to removing a fitting underneath the running plate of this Black 5. This was hot and dirty and, at times, dangerous work.

Always looking for that unusual viewpoint, Colin Garratt's photographic art is ably demonstrated in this view, which he christened "Rust & Burnt Umber", detailing a rusting Black 5 glimpsed through the charred remains of a wooden bodied goods van. The conveniently seeded intervening sapling adds interest to the image.

A pair of Black 5s, the identity of the furthest locomotive not being discernible in the absence of the cabside, await their fate whilst the scrapman turns his attention to the connecting rods. The yard had a reputation for being difficult to access even when cutting was not taking place. This was evidenced by the fact that when an RCTS party arrived at the yard by DMU on 18th May 1968, on a tour that included a trip on the adjacent Loddington branch, they were warned in advance that they would not be welcome and that a reception party of two men and a dog awaited them! In the event this threat did not materialise and tour participants were allowed to wander round the scrapyard. It says much for Colin Garratt's persuasive powers etc.

A Class 101 DMU is seen inside the famous, or should that be infamous, incinerator at Mayer Newman's breakers yard prior to the shutter being lowered and the fire ignited. This process burnt away all the flammable material in an enclosed environment prior to subsequent cutting up. This was an effective way of reducing the expense involved in scrapping railway vehicles as the greatest costs were normally incurred in the removal of all non-metallic parts such as interior seats and panelling. Meyer Newman came up with this novel approach at Snailwell causing the entire vehicle to be incinerated, leaving only a twisted and warped shell which could then easily be cut into manageable sections.

Class 302 Electric Multiple Unit No. 253, one of the fleet built for the London, Tilbury & Southend line between 1958-60, gets the heat treatment in the firing tunnel. The rundown of the class began in 1984 with the majority being phased out when the Class 310s were introduced on to the LT&S line in 1988 with the last 30 units being withdrawn by 1998. Following firing the charred remains would then be dragged out of the incinerator for cutting prior to onward transmission for reprocessing.

A similar process is about to engulf former Hastings DMU No. 1034. These 6B units had cost £90,860 each when new in 1958 and were similar to the 6S and 6L units except that an unclassified buffet car replaced one of the second class carriages. This unit was withdrawn in April 1986 and then stored at a variety of locations. Final destruction of the motor cars of the unit did not take place at Snailwell until June 1990.

The intense heat generated was sufficient to melt sections of the front panels of the DMU as illustrated here. A vision of Hades indeed!

Like the daubs of some modern painting, the scorched and rusted paintwork of a DMU presented a suitable canvas for Colin Garratt's photographic eye to capture on film.

Following burning in the incinerator, the metal frames of the former seating are jumbled inside the remaining shell of the centre car of this DMU, which still sports its twin silencers, prior to towing out into the yard for cutting to take place.

The rusting remains of a DMU lie in the yard as the scrapman in checked shirt gets to work with his cutting torch inside the shell of the unit. Rather like Cohen's this yard was in a rural setting as the tall fir trees seen in the background testify.

Like the sword of Damocles hanging over it, the crane grab arm is about to lift the front section of a DMU onto the pile of assorted scrap seen in the background.

Awaiting its turn for incineration, an unidentified 3H Hampshire, later Class 205, "Thumper" DMU is parked on a siding. As an aid to platform staff the black triangle seen on the front indicated which end of the unit contained the guard's compartment. The engines of all motor car units were removed prior to incineration.

An example of the sign writer's art is shown in this close up of the unit details of the Class 205 DMU indicating its tare weight and overall length and width given in good old feet and inches. As can be seen, the driving units were 56 tons (DMBSO) whilst the trailers were 30 tons (TS) and 32 tons (DTC). The peeling paint adds to the air of abandonment captured in this image.

Vic Berry - Leicester

The famous stack of locomotive body shells was a much photographed feature of Vic Berry's Leicester yard and in this view eighteen bodies can be seen consisting primarily of Class 25s and Class 27s. Withdrawal of the final examples of the Class 25 had occurred in 1987 and with scrapping having come to an end the previous year at Swindon, upon closure of the works, and with re-organisation at the other in-house scrapping facility at Doncaster, Vic Berry became involved in the cutting of the final examples.

Using a fish-eye lens enabled Colin Garratt to capture the locomotive stack from below to give an enhanced sense of the impressive scale of the pile. The stack had been initiated to make much needed space in the yard as some 50 examples of Class 25s had arrived during the summer of 1987, such that it became necessary to strip them of their bogies and engines and stack the body shells until such time as they could be attended to. Amazingly quite a few of the cab windows remained seemingly undamaged by this process.

A pile of Class 25 cabs await processing amongst which are Nos. 25 133, 25 051 and 25 224. No. 25 051 had been withdrawn from Carlisle Kingmoor in June 1985 and was stored there until March 1987. Travelling via Crewe and Bescot, it arrived at Vic Berry's yard on 12th March with cutting commencing promptly on 1st. April. However, the bogies from this locomotive were returned to BR for use in one of the ETHEL (Electric Train Heating Ex Locomotive) units based at Marylebone, No. 97252, to replace those on the principal donor locomotive No. 25 314.

Amongst this pile of assorted cabs, Nos. 25 158 and 25 190 can be identified. There is also a Class 45 cab and a couple of cabs from unidentified Class 40s in the mix. In 1987 for example, five of the latter class arrived at the yard intact and in addition three cabs were sent from Swindon Works for asbestos removal. The River Soar flows past this spot and it was one of the most polluted rivers in the country, taking on a pinkish hue due to discharges from industry, predominantly textile mills. Today the river flowing through Leicester is much cleaner.

Some rolling stock bogies were recovered and returned to BR for further use but that doesn't seem likely to be the fate of this example already missing one of its wheels and after further cutting will surely join the pile of miscellaneous scrap seen in the background. The axlebox of the wheelset in the foreground is marked BR Hoffman, the firm of Hoffman being based at Chelmsford. This was the UK's first ball bearing factory established in 1898 by cousins Geoffrey and Charles Barrett and financed by American ball bearing machine manufacturer Ernst Gustav Hoffmann from whom the Company took its name. The factory, which finally closed in 1989, was a supplier not just to the railway industry but also produced bearings for automobiles, aircraft and the war effort.

BR
METRO-CAMMELL
Lot No 30249
1956

This builder's plate came from one of many Class 101 DMUs which were built by Metro-Cammell at Washwood Heath Locomotive Works in Birmingham between 1956 and 1959. The class proved to be one of the most successful and longest surviving of all BR's first generation DMUs with the final five units not being withdrawn until December 2003, by which time the oldest set had been in service for 47 years. Lot No. 30249, recorded on this plate, dates from 1956.

Colin Garratt's fascination with severed wheels seems to have accompanied him to Leicester where this shot of wheels encrusted in grime reflected in rainwater makes for a pleasing composition.

The accommodation may have been for first class travellers only as the sign indicates but businessmen would no doubt baulk at travelling in this vehicle in its present state with its windows smashed. Colin Garratt was attracted by the photographic possibilities of close up images and this one is undoubtedly enhanced by the crazing of the safety glass.

What could possibly pass as a piece of modern sculpture - might this perhaps be entitled "Scrap symphony with springs".

Bright metal is still apparent on the cogs of the gear wheels and on the severed axles in contrast to the dull sheen and rust apparent on those parts of the wheels normally exposed to the environment.

With the English propensity for peculiar collective nouns such as a parliament of rooks and a wisdom of owls, I'm not sure what the collective noun for sets of bogies might be – perhaps a "commonwealth of bogies" might suit – here is such a collection substantially complete with springs, torsion bars, etc. stacked one on the other.

With gloves, helmet and visor in place, the scrapman gets to work with his torch producing a fine display of sparks. In the background is Mark 1 coach M18840 and although construction of this type of vehicle ended in 1963, multiple units and non-passenger carrying stock based on the Mark 1 design continued to be built until 1974. However, by the late 1990s the Mark 1 began to reach the end of its design life and concerns about its safety relative to newer stock became more pressing, leading to the withdrawal of locomotive hauled vehicles. Although originally numbered in the 25XXX series, stock was renumbered in the 18XXX series from 1983 with this example built by Metro-Cammell dating from 1957.

This mechanical excavator seems to have embedded itself in this pile of miscellaneous scrap. Whether it was one of Berry's own life expired machines or not is unknown but its condition looks pretty terminal.

Piles of seat frames from DMUs occupy the foreground, the upholstery and cushions no doubt having already been burnt off as being of no salvageable value.

One of Vic Berry's caterpillar tracked mobile cranes seen in the background to this shot is a reminder that a considerable quantity of plant, in addition to just cutting tools and gas cylinders, was required in such an operation in order to transport items to and from the scrapyard and to position them once on site.

The potentially dangerous nature of some of the cutting operations undertaken is amply demonstrated in this view of a cutter perched nonchalantly upon the roof of a Class 33. Like a woodsman lopping a tree, one has to be sure (no doubt) not to cut away the branch you are sitting on!

A red Welsh dragon adorns the front of this 3 car Suburban Class 116 DMU No. C301, formerly operating on the South Wales valley lines. In February 1985 No. C334 became the first such set to be adorned with Valley Trains markings that involved a red Welsh dragon under the centre cab window in between a thin red line forming a V, which then continued horizontally under the other cab windows. Under the first passenger window on each side of the unit was a small BR logo and a white Welsh dragon. On the non-driver side these were accompanied by the text 'Tren y Cym', Welsh for 'Valley Train'. These units were introduced to South Wales in December 1957 and operated there until the final unit was withdrawn from the principality in September 1992. Upon arrival in the yard DMUs usually proceeded first to a pre-stripping shed where all internal fittings such as luggage racks would be removed.

Seen through the chain link fencing that surrounded much of the yard, the most interesting items are a couple of former London Transport Underground coaches of CO/CP stock dating from the late 1930s.

With vegetation seemingly about to overwhelm the yard fencing, the stacks of coach bodies reveal a further ex-LT Underground coach behind which, on the top of the stack, are a couple of Mark 1 coaches marked Motorail which was a BR long distance service provided to ferry cars and their passengers to and from a variety of destinations. Originating as a brand in 1966, the service, having run at a loss for some years, finished in 1995 upon privatisation. First Great Western re-launched a similar service, using GUV vans, as part of its overnight Night Riviera from Paddington to Penzance but this was withdrawn in 2005.

The mass of wiring and piping that constituted the "innards" of a Class 33 are revealed as the ventilation grilles receive the attention of the scrapman whilst another operative attacks the front end.

This shot reveals the detail of the type of torch used by the yard to cut metal. With most of the locomotive body already removed, attention has turned to detaching the buffers. It says much for Colin Garratt's persuasive powers that he was allowed to get so close to the action in what, by today's standards, would be considered a dangerous environment such that the general public would surely be excluded or severely restricted in their ability to wander around such a yard whilst cutting was taking place.

Against a background of a stack of a variety of coaching stock, including a DMU and an SR electric 4TC unit, No. 2806, a couple of workmen get to grips with half a Class 33 whose cabside number has already been removed, no doubt for resale to enthusiasts. Close examination reveals that a couple of the coaches in the stack carry the legend VB meaning that they were vacuum rather than air braked.

In addition to propane torches, angle grinders were an essential item of kit for scrapyards and one is seen in action here in this busy scene where no fewer than four workers are engaged in reducing a once proud locomotive to scrap.

This close up reveals the BOC red propane gas cylinders along with a supply of black oxygen cylinders. It is the mixture of these two gases which powers the cutting torches. BOC is a multinational British based industrial gas company now part of Linde plc. BOC did not originally stand for British Oxygen Co., as many might think, but Brin's Oxygen Company which was originally formed in 1886 by two French brothers, Arthur and Leon Brin. In 1906 the firm was renamed British Oxygen Co., becoming the BOC Group in 1978 with the acquisition of an American competitor.

Bogies produced much of the valuable tonnage of high-grade steel released through dismantling locomotives and, as such, bogie cutting was a prolific activity in any railway scrapyard. In a cascade of fire and sparks, the scrapman is intent on separating the wheels from the bogie frame.

This pile of buffers obviously caught Colin Garratt's eye as having the potential to make a suitably pleasing photographic composition. The majority of the buffers are stamped OLEO which is a company whose current publicity advises that they "Lead the world in energy absorption". Oleo began when the original Oleo Pneumatics shock absorber was developed from the Vickers gun recuperative gear design which was first applied to an aeroplane by a French company, Breguet Aviation. The innovation behind the original design, patented by Vickers Armstrong in 1915, was recoil control achieved by forcing oil through orifices in a positive manner. For many years this principle of energy absorption was developed for the aviation industry for fixed undercarriages. This led on to the development of the hydraulic railway buffer, the patent for which was lodged by Peter Thornhill in 1951, thereby pioneering the first practical design for a self-contained hydraulic buffer for railway rolling stock.

Piled four high, this image captures the impressive nature of the stack of coaches that had built up at Berry's yard. The inscription "No Brakes" can be seen adorning the side of W24888 which would appear to be the least of its worries given its current position.

An intriguing viewpoint taken from the inside of a locomotive body shell looking up through the roof to a Class 25 atop the stack. The canisters on the right still carry endorsements such as "Anti slip" and "Goods, Passenger Changeover Vac" and "Goods Passenger Changeover Air", presumably as an aid to drivers and/or maintenance staff.

A somewhat vertiginous view looking up the teetering cliffside of the coaching stack, remarkably there were no reports of any collapses of these stacks over the years. A number of Mark 1 and 2 coaches are marked with the code C1, a clearance code, indicating that they are 20m in length. The former SK (Corridor Second) on the right also carries the designation ETH indicating electric train heating.

As withdrawn coaching stock often spent long periods in store on sidings, they were prone to the attentions of graffiti artists and these examples certainly seem to have suffered, although I don't think Banksy has anything to worry about! In the foreground is GUV (General Utility Vehicle) NKV M93876, one of over 900 of this type constructed during the period 1956-60.

Some very distressed looking coaches adorn the stack, the parlous state of some being possibly due to accident damage sustained in traffic rather than that inflicted at the scrapyard. The Mark 3 coach in the left foreground seems to have been particularly badly affected.

A former Isle of Wight ex-LT Underground unit sporting its Ryde Rail insignia and (NSE) Network SouthEast livery sits astride a couple of Inter City Sleepers. This was one of the 5 car units with the end door plated over, a number of which ended their days at Vic Berry's yard after journeying by road from Fratton following transfer by ferry back to the mainland.

"Hooray and up she rises" - It took two cranes working in harmony to lift coach bodies onto the stacks and in this view a former Southern Region First Class Mark 1 vehicle is being manoeuvred into position whilst on the right ex SR EMU No. 8020 of Class 458 awaits its fate.

Some Scottish Region Class 27s were adorned with a West Highland Terrier logo and here No. 27 038, originally numbered D5390, is captured in the yard having arrived in August 1987 following withdrawal in February. The first twenty-three members of the class had been delivered to the ScR in 1961/2 and went initially to replace steam on the West Highland line. The canine logo was apparently devised by Eastfield Depot in Glasgow with a stag, a castle and a salmon being used by other Area Maintenance Engineers. Damage to the locomotive roof is clearly visible, probably resulting from engine removal.

A view of the cab interior of a Class 27 shows the 90 mph speed restriction, the former front communicating door and the amazingly well preserved set of dials and controls seemingly pretty well undamaged. The window glass on the left has gone however leaving the rubber strip surrounds hanging whilst the former windscreen wipers now perform no useful function. The "SSF" marking visible underneath the speed restriction indicates Speed Sensing Fitted which was a device which applied the brakes should the driver select 'Engine Only' or 'Off' on the direction selector when the locomotive was in motion. Should the locomotive run away unattended, this same device detected this and applied the brakes.

"I wonder what this bit is from?" A trio of camera toting enthusiasts wander round the yard, no doubt trying to identify miscellaneous items lying about the site.

A scrapman sets about a bogie in order to reduce it to manageable chunks for subsequent melting down in the scrap furnaces where it will no doubt be recycled into something quite different. In the background is GUV No. NKV M93509, this example having been used primarily for mail traffic. This was one of many such freight vehicles which Vic Berry's yard handled in addition to locomotives, multiple units and coaches.

As is apparent from this pile of scrap, it was not just railway items that were dealt with at Berry's. A fine assortment of cars, M, R and W suffix numberplates of which can be discerned dating from 1973, 1976 and 1980 respectively. I wonder if any readers can identify their own cherished vehicle.

A contrast in light and shade reveals this pyrotechnic display resulting from the cutting activities of one of Vic Berry's workmen applying his torch to the side of an unidentified Class 33.

Scrapyards were no respecters even of Pullman cars. A brace of them are seen here behind a pile of buffers awaiting the final indignity, their days of providing luxury travel well and truly behind them.

Today flame-cut numbers sell for several hundreds of pounds on the railwayana market and Vic Berry was undoubtedly aware that enthusiasts were willing to pay handsomely for such trophies. I believe he generally charged about £100-£150 back in the 1990s. Whilst admittedly not having the allure of steam locomotive numberplates, they became increasingly sought after as the diesel fleet was withdrawn. Here a flame cut section of Class 47 No. 47 113 awaits a new home amongst a sea of debris and the remains of a Class 33. Withdrawn from service in January 1988, 47 113 was broken up here in September 1990, one of about 20 of the class that passed through the Leicester site.

With the feet of the scrapman visible in the top right of the picture, his cutting activities produce a shower of sparks cascading down the front of the victim caught by Colin Garratt's camera, no doubt using a fast shutter speed. Note the electrical connections hanging loose on the left of this shot.

The impressive former Great Central Railway Goods warehouse, with its logo just about readable, forms the backdrop to this view of one of Vic Berry's vehicles, its cab endorsed with the firm's name and location – Western Boulevard Leicester. The firm's road fleet was used both to carry away recovered scrap and to deliver cabs from locomotives cut off site for their asbestos to be removed.

Against a desolate wasteland in the foreground, the horizontal stacks of DMUs, one of which carries the legend Valley Train, are complemented in this image by the verticals of the yard crane and one of the many factory chimneys that could be seen in Leicester at that time, in the distance on the other side of the former GCR tracks that ran adjacent to the site.

An unidentified pair of Class 33s lie side by side, each exhibiting similar incisions into the cab front bodywork, presumably to extract some valuable item. "Flying cutters", i.e. staff from Vic Berry, had been active at Eastleigh Works in cutting four members of the class in 1989/90 whilst nine examples comprised the final locomotive deliveries to the Leicester yard with six arriving in September and three in November 1990.

As mentioned earlier, power units and bogies were stripped from newly arrived locomotives to enable their body shells to be stacked, thus freeing space in the yard. The engine from one such unit occupies the foreground in this shot which also shows a further example of a former Scottish Region Class 27, No. 27 052, with West Highland Terrier logo, on the right, whilst a couple of severed cab units from the same class are also apparent. An Eastern Region DMBC (Driving Motor Brake Composite) coach, E51825, from a Class 110 DMU can be identified in the background. This unit did go on to some form of immortality, albeit in miniature, as it was modelled by Hornby as their 00 gauge 3 car set.

Our final view of Vic Berry's yard shows a stack of some of the Isle of Wight Standard Underground stock coaches in the striking Network SouthEast livery demonstrating why perhaps it was known to enthusiasts as "toothpaste stripe". Some sixteen DMBS and CT/TS coaches were taken by low loader to Leicester from storage at either Fratton or Ruislip.